Along Came Galileo

written and illustrated
by JEANNE BENDICK

Beautiful Feet Books
San Luis Obispo, California

Cover Art by Jeanne Bendick
Design and Layout by Jesse McKay

Published by Beautiful Feet Books
1306 Mill Street
San Luis Obispo, CA 93401

www.bfbooks.com
800.889.1978

Contents

Introduction

Out of the wonderful, changing and reawakening world of the Renaissance came Galileo Galelei, one of the most important and fascinating scientists of all time. Through his eyes the world would come to see and understand things of which they had never dreamed. His discoveries unlocked truths of the universe which challenged commonly held scientific and religious thought.

It was Galileo's questioning mind and insatiable curiousity which drove him to monumental breakthroughs in astronomy, physics, mechanics and the natural world. He believed that, "Doubt is the father of invention, opening the way to the discovery of truth." His delight in his discoveries and his eagerness to share them have left us with a rich legacy of writings which, 350 years later, are understandable to any literate reader.

One remarkable aspect of Galileo's life was that he was very much a man of faith as well as science. Even while developing and establishing the scientific method, he believed firmly in the truth of scripture. He felt that the languages of religion and science should not be used to define each other. He said, "God is a Spirit. From His Divine word, Holy Scripture and Nature do alike proceed. I think in discussing Nature we ought not to begin with texts from the Scripture, but with experiment and demonstration. The Holy Scriptures cannot err, but its interpreters can." Sadly, Galileo was far ahead of his times and he suffered much injustice for daring to speak those things he knew to be true.

Galileo's contributions to the world of science include his discoveries in astronomy, physics and mathematics. He perfected the first astronomical telescope and a compound microscope. He wrote laws about falling bodies and floating bodies. He measured the rotation of the sun. He invented a thermometer; a geometrical compass; a pendulum clock and a way to test precious metals. He got great pleasure from applying his scientific knowledge to the problems of local tradesmen. He was also a lover of art and an accomplished artist himself; he played the lute and enjoyed working in his garden. Galileo was truly a Renaissance man.

He was the first to see, through the lens of his telescope, the wonders of our galaxy. During these times he was filled with a profound sense of awe and gratitude. "Therefore do I give thanks to God who has been pleased to make me the first observer of marvelous things that were unrevealed to bygone days."

Galileo was often referred to as the "Archimedes of his Time," because of his discoveries in mathematics, mechanics and astronomy. It is fitting that Jeanne Bendick, who so successfully depicted Archimedes' life in her book, *Archimedes and the Door of Science*, should follow that wonderful work with this insightful and delightful look into the life of a courageous man of faith and science.

Rea Coleen Berg

Sandwich, Massachusetts, 1999

ALONG CAME GALILEO

(1)

Along Came Galileo

On February 15, 1564, a boy named Galileo Galilei was born in the city of Pisa in Italy.

At the time Galileo was born, most people believed that they could see and feel what the world was like and how it worked. You could look up and watch the sun move across the sky, so the sun must be going around the earth. You could feel that the earth under your feet didn't move. It was common sense to believe that these things were true.

Almost everyone accepted the ideas of the ancient Greek thinkers, who had lived fifteen centuries before.

When Galileo Galilei was born, a little more than four hundred years ago, most people believed that the universe looked like this.

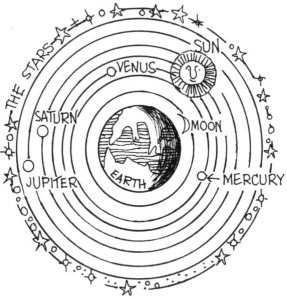

The earth was in the center of everything. The earth stood still. The sun, the moon and the five planets known to the ancient world all revolved in circles around the earth. Beyond planet Saturn were the stars, fixed in place in a slowly-turning dome.

And that was the whole universe.

Today we know that the sun is in the center of a group of nine planets that revolve around it. The earth is one of those planets. Some planets have moons that revolve around them. The sun, the planets and their moons make up our solar system.

Now we know that our solar system is only a very small part of our galaxy, the Milky Way. And our galaxy is only one of the billions of galaxies in the universe.

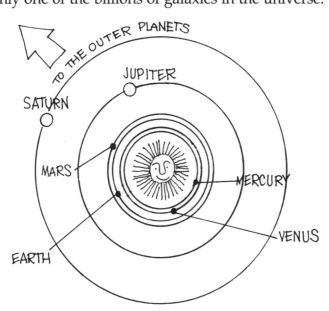

You can see that these two ideas about the universe are very different.

The old picture of the universe hadn't changed for 1,500 years.

Then, along came Galileo.

Many people think that Galileo was the first modern scientist.

He understood that science is full of surprises. He challenged ideas that most people believed about the world. He said that you couldn't just believe an idea because it seemed to be true. He said that ideas must be tested, to prove them true or false.

He experimented with moving objects, to see what happened when they fell, rolled, floated or were pushed. He experimented with magnetism and gravity, even though nobody knew what those things were. He experimented with air.

ALONG CAME GALILEO

Galileo wrote letters, books and papers, explaining his ideas. He made rules for writing about science: Be clear. Say only what's important. Write well enough so that everyone — not only scientists — can understand the subject.

He invented a thermometer, a calculating instrument, an instrument for measuring time, a machine for irrigating fields and a weighing machine for testing precious metals. He invented a microscope.

He took glass lenses, which people had been using for hundreds of years, and put them together to make a telescope for looking at the heavens.

Looking through his telescope, Galileo was the first person to see the sun, the moon, the planets and the stars as they really are.

He said that we must be ready to change old ideas as we learn new facts.

Galileo fought to make scientists free to express their ideas.

 **Galileo said:** *Language is the seal of all the inventions of mankind, speaking to those who are not yet born and who will not be born for a thousand or ten thousand years.*

PISA

VENICE

PADUA

FLORENCE

ROME

NAPLES

(2)

Galileo's World

At the time Galileo was born, Italy was not a single country as it is now. It was a jumble of independent city-states. Each city-state had at least one large and prosperous city with towns and farmlands around it. All the city-states had one thing in common — the Catholic religion. Everywhere the Church was very powerful.

Important princes and their families ruled those city-states which were so rich and beautiful that some European countries fought battles to control them. (The cities also fought among themselves. The city of Pisa, where Galileo was born, had been taken over by the city-state of Florence.)

Galileo was born toward the end of a time in Europe called the Renaissance. In the years between 1400 and 1600 there was an explosion of writing, painting, sculpture, architecture, design and new ideas.

Italy was a center of the Renaissance. In the cities where Galileo grew up, he could see wonderful things almost anywhere he walked.

Architects had designed grand buildings, set in enormous open squares. There were statues and fountains. Inside, the palaces and churches were decorated with beautiful paintings.

In their shops, craftsmen worked in gold and silver. They carved furniture, sewed elegant clothes and embroidered tapestries.

Writers in the cities wrote poems and plays. Musicians composed music. Scholars studied and taught in famous universities.

All these things were supported by the important families and the Church, who got their money by taxing the merchants, the farmers and the ordinary citizens.

Galileo's family wasn't rich but they lived comfortably.

Most people were poor and uneducated. Families lived in one or two small rooms, their houses crowded together on narrow streets.

Windows had shutters, but no glass. Houses had no running water. Wood was used for cooking, in a fireplace or maybe a stove. Some people had to take their food to a baker, to be cooked in his oven. Candles provided light but they were very expensive, so most people went to bed when it got dark.

The great squares of the city were paved, but streets in the poor sections were only dirt and stones. There were open sewers. Nobody had invented refrigeration or a way of keeping food from spoiling. Nobody knew, yet, what caused diseases.

As soon as boys were old enough, they were apprenticed to different kinds of tradesmen so they could learn a skill to earn a living. They worked (without pay) for carpenters or blacksmiths, shoemakers, butchers or bakers, until they learned their trade.

A master took a boy into his household for years, giving him food and clothes, teaching him and punishing him when he thought he should. At the end of his training the master tested his apprentice to be sure he had learned well. Then he became a journeyman, working in his own trade.

Boys who showed artistic talent were apprenticed to artists and craftsmen. Usually, girls stayed at home, learning to spin and sew and cook. Almost everything a poor family needed was made at home.

The idea that even poor children should go to school, at least for a while, was beginning to catch on. At first there were only Sunday schools, where children were taught religion, good habits and how to read and write.

Gradually, especially in towns and cities, the Church established schools for teaching the children of poor families. Most of the students were boys. Reading was not supposed to be of any use to poor girls. Schools for poor children were serious. There was no time for play or sports in school, but in the streets and squares children played stick ball, leapfrog and tug-of-war. They rolled hoops, balls and marbles, they juggled and flew kites. Boys wrestled and pretended to be soldiers.

Important families and those with money educated their children in a different way.

The Galilei family was well-known in Florence, one of the richest, most powerful city-states. Galileo's father, Vincenzio, had moved from Florence to Pisa, where he was married to a rather bad-tempered woman named Julia Ammanati. In 1564 Galileo was born. Nine years later his sister Virginia was born; then his brother Michelangelo. (Not the famous artist, Michelangelo, who died the year Galileo was born.) Then came a sister, Livia. (Records say that there was another brother and two other sisters, but nobody knows what happened to them.)

When Galileo was ten, the family moved back to Florence.

Vincenzio Galilei was a fine musician. He played the lute and he wrote music. But music was not

enough to support his family, so he was also a cloth merchant.

Vincenzio was much more interested in mathematics and music than he was in buying and selling cloth. He taught Galileo to read and to play the lute and the organ. He hired a teacher to come to the house and teach Galileo about the ancient Greek thinkers. So Galileo began to learn the geometry of Archimedes and Euclid; the astronomy of Ptolemy; and Aristotle's ideas about the natural world.

When Galileo was eleven, he was sent to boarding school in a monastery at Vallombrosa, to study Latin, Greek, music, drawing and geometry.

Galileo loved music and played the lute all his life. He wanted to be a musician, but Vincenzio was afraid

Galileo would never be able to earn a living as a musician. He was determined that Galileo would be a doctor.

When he was seventeen, Galileo began studying
medicine at the University of Pisa.

Galileo said: *Doubt is the father of
invention, opening the way to the
discovery of truth.*

(3)

Galileo Goes to College

At the end of the 16th century, four hundred years ago, colleges were not like they are now. The University of Pisa was not a place where new ideas were taught or encouraged. The ancient Greek thinkers, who had lived more than 1,500 years before, were supposed to have known, or discovered, all the true ideas about the world and how it worked. Being educated meant studying what they believed.

It's as if now, when you went to school, you learned only what people knew 1,500 years ago.

You wouldn't learn about atoms or electricity or

14

gravity. You wouldn't know about other continents than the one you live on. You wouldn't learn about space or galaxies or the universe, or what the earth was like beneath your feet or what caused the weather to change.

You wouldn't know what made people sick or how to cure them. You wouldn't have the knowledge to even think about inventing the thousands of things that are part of our everyday world, now.

It is true that the ancient Greek wise men were amazing. Their ideas were not based on things other people had discovered before them. They had to think about things from the beginning.

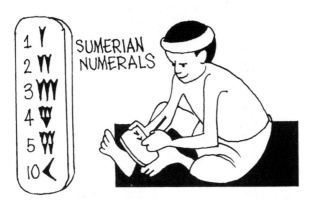

All the ancient people — not only the Greeks, but the Egyptians before them, and the Sumerians before them had brilliant ideas. The Sumerians invented writing. The Egyptians used astronomy to invent a calendar and to predict the flooding of the Nile River.

They used geometry to measure land and to build the pyramids.

But the Greeks asked the most questions. (They thought that questions were more important than answers.)

What were they seeing when they looked up at the heavens? What was earth's place in the universe? What was everything made of? Why did things fall, move or stop, float or sink? Could time be measured? How big was the sun? How far were the stars?

Their answers were inspired. The mathematician, Euclid, wrote thirteen books on geometry. Euclid's geometry is still used for our calculations of actual things. (We need other kinds of geometry for understanding time and space, energy and what goes on inside atoms.)

Eratosthenes measured the circumference of the earth and the sizes and distances of the sun and the moon.

In the fifth century BC Democritus suggested that all matter was made of separate particles, which he called atoms.

Over hundreds of years the Greeks thought and argued and wrote down their ideas. They were so thoughtful, and they wrote so clearly, that very few people disputed those ideas for fifteen centuries.

Experimenting wasn't important to most of the Greeks. They figured out what the world was like by observation. For most of them, seeing was believing. The Greeks called their observations of how the world works, Natural Philosophy.

(Philosophy is the study of human knowledge — what people believe, how we think and how we know the things we know.)

We call observing and testing our ideas of how the world works, science.

In Galileo's life, the most important of the ancient Greeks was Aristotle, who lived from 384 to 322 BC.

Aristotle was one of the great thinkers of all time. He was an original thinker, which means that his ideas were not based on the ideas or discoveries of the

ARISTOTLE· HOW HE THOUGHT THE WORLD WAS.
(NOBODY REALLY KNOWS WHAT THOSE
ANCIENT SCIENTISTS LOOKED LIKE.)

people who lived before him. Even though he had mastered all the knowledge of the Greeks to his time, there was still a world of things to learn.

Aristotle's teacher, the Greek philosopher, Plato, gave him a way of thinking. (Aristotle was a teacher, too. His most famous pupil was Alexander the Great, who later conquered the whole known world.)

Aristotle studied nature. He made careful observations of plants and animals. His classifications of living things were wonderfully accurate.

He believed that the world was made of earth and water, air and fire. Earth was our planet, the unmoving center of the universe. Over earth was the water of the seas. Air was over the water and over air was fire, which reached to the moon.

18

Aristotle said that the celestial bodies were made of something different than earth stuff because they glowed, while objects on earth had no light. (He called the mysterious, glowing stuff "aether.")

Aristotle taught that there were two natural motions: down, belonging to earth and water, and up, belonging to air and fire. He said that all other motions were "unnatural."

He said that God was responsible for all motion.

Aristotle taught that all human knowledge begins with the senses. What your senses tell you is always true.

The Greeks called the universe the Cosmos , which meant an orderly and harmonious arrangement. Aristotle believed that the universe was complete and perfect. Every part of it was eternal and unchanging.

(For most of Galileo's life, Aristotle was going to cause him trouble.)

Claudius Ptolemy, who lived from the year 90 until 168, was the last of the great Greek astronomers. He put together the work of all the Greek astronomers who came before him and cataloged the known stars.

The Almagest, his writings on astronomy, was the only important reference in astronomy for 1,400 years.

Ptolemy's plan of the universe showed the earth as a globe in the center of the heavens, with the sun, moon, planets and stars revolving around it, each in an immense, crystal sphere.

(Ptolemy's geography was no longer taught by

UNKNOWN

UNKNOWN

WESTERN OCEAN

TO CHINA →

AFRICA

INDIA

UNKNOWN

PTOLEMY· AND ONE OF HIS MAPS OF THE WORLD

Galileo's time, because the New World had been discovered.)

Archimedes, who lived from 287 until 212 BC, was Galileo's favorite Greek. He was a mathematician, an inventor and a physicist. (Physics is the study of matter and energy.) Archimedes believed in thinking things through, step by step, and figuring out experiments to prove his ideas.

He proved that with a lever he could move almost anything.

He found a way to tell different substances apart by their density — how heavy they were.

He experimented with liquids to find why some things float and others sink.

He proved that there is no end to numbers.

Something important happened to Galileo during one of his vacations from the University. Ostilio Ricci,

ARCHIMEDES •
INVENTED A WAY TO MEASURE THE ANGLES
OF THE RISING SUN.

a family friend and Professor of Mathematics at the court of the Duke of Tuscany, (the local ruler) agreed to give him lessons in mathematics. Ricci taught mathematics not just as numbers, but as a useful way to help solve science problems. Archimedes was a favorite of his, too.

Galileo was so happy in his study of mathematics with Professor Ricci that his father gave him permission to continue the lessons, as long as they did not interfere with his study of medicine.

Medicine at the University was mostly a study of the work of another ancient Greek, Galen, who lived from the year 130 until 200.

For all the years since then, Galen had been the great authority on medicine. He had proved that arteries carried blood, not air. He wrote about nerves and the brain,

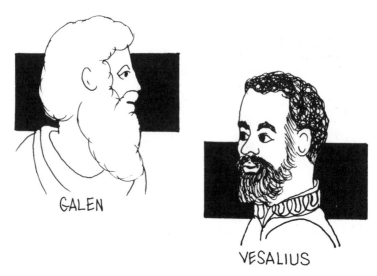

GALEN

VESALIUS

about the spine and the pulse. He wrote about the history of medicine and about his experiments on animals. In Galileo's time, very few doctors or professors questioned Galen's ideas. New investigations in medicine were discouraged. (Andreas Vesalius, who taught at the University of Padua from 1537 to 1546, had made important discoveries about anatomy that disagreed with Galen. He was so criticized for challenging Galen's work that he left the university and Italy.)

If you were sick, a doctor might take out some of your blood with a leech. He might set a broken bone or chop away an infected part. Probably, though, you went to an apothecary — what we call a pharmacist now — to get medicine. Maybe the medicine was a dose of strange mixtures to swallow. Or maybe it was herbs, burned to release their smell. Fir cones and

branches, wormwood, oak, lavender, cooking herbs and tobacco smoke were all supposed to be helpful.

Nobody at the University questioned the ideas of the ancient Greeks, or argued about them. Except Galileo.

The professors regarded him as a trouble maker. He had lost all interest in medicine. Besides, his father was running out of money. So in 1585, without earning a degree, Galileo left the University.

 **Galileo said:** *I do not believe that the same God who has endowed us with senses, reason and intellect has intended us to forego their use.*

GALILEO AND THE SWINGING LAMP

One day, while he was a student, Galileo stood in the drafty Cathedral at Pisa and watched a lamp swinging on a long chain. The lamp would make a big swing. Then the swing would get smaller. Galileo decided to time the swings. (How did he do that? Clocks hadn't been invented yet.)

Galileo used the beat of his pulse. (If you are healthy, your pulse is as regular as the tick of a clock.) He found out that each complete swing, whether the arc was big or small, took the same amount of time.

Later, he experimented himself, using a weight on a long chain. It was true. A small swing took the same time as a big swing.

You can try this, with a yo-yo.

Let the string of the yo-yo all the way out. Have someone start the yo-yo swinging with a big push. Time the swing from the place it started until it swings back to that place. The swings will get smaller and smaller. Time those swings, too. (You can count the ticks of a clock to time the swings. Or you can count the beats of your pulse.) What have you found out?

Galileo knew he had discovered something important. It was the idea of a pendulum. But he didn't connect that with the idea of using a pendulum to regulate a clock for about fifty years.

(4)

Galileo Becomes a Professor

For the next four years, Galileo was at home with his family. He studied and he wrote; he tutored in mathematics and did some lecturing. And he began inventing. One of his inventions, the hydrostatic balance, was based on Archimedes' idea for identifying different kinds of metals that had been made into objects. Were the objects pure gold? Was the gold mixed with silver or other metals? You couldn't tell by looking, but the value of an object depended on the answer.

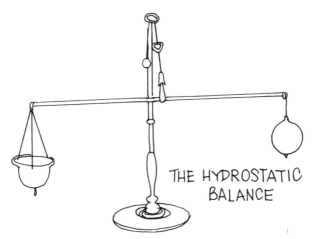

THE HYDROSTATIC
BALANCE

The hydrostatic balance made him some money, but all the things he was doing still weren't enough to make a living. It was discouraging. He even wondered if he should give up science and try to make his fortune in the Orient.

Then, in 1589, important family friends recommended him to the Grand Duke of Tuscany, who granted him a three year position as Professor of Mathematics at the University of Pisa, even though he had never graduated from that university. (Grand Dukes were important people.)

Galileo's salary was 60 scudi a year. In today's money, that would be about $30 a week. Everything was much, much cheaper in those times, but still, that wasn't really enough to support himself and help his family. Galileo needed more money, so he spent a lot of his time tutoring students at the university. He taught them Euclid's geometry, Ptolemy's astronomy and Aristotle's theory of motion —his ideas about why and how things moved.

But Galileo questioned Aristotle's theory that all heavier things fall to earth faster than lighter things do. He argued the idea with the other professors, who laughed at him. Galileo was determined to prove that Aristotle's idea was wrong.

The story is that one day, with an audience of students and professors, he climbed to the top of the Leaning Tower of Pisa with two cannon balls. One weighed one pound; the other weighed ten pounds. He dropped them both at exactly the same time and they landed at exactly the same time. (Of course if he had dropped a cannon ball and a blanket, the result would have been different. Why, do you think?)

Even though they had watched the experiment, the other professors didn't believe what they saw. They were furious with Galileo for challenging Aristotle's ideas.

Galileo used another experiment to prove that another of Aristotle's ideas was wrong.

Aristotle thought that things fell down because they had weight. If things didn't fall, it meant they had no weight. Since air didn't fall, Aristotle said that it had no weight.

Galileo pumped air into a bladder — a sort of balloon made of animal skin. He sealed the bladder and weighed it. Then he punctured the bladder to let the air out and weighed it again. Now, the bladder weighed less, so Galileo proved that air has weight, even though it doesn't fall.

In his lectures, Galileo began to make fun of the other professors for their closed minds. The students loved him and the other professors hated him more and more. They came to his lectures and hissed at his ideas.

In 1591 Vincenzio Galilei died. Now, Galileo was responsible for supporting the whole family. It was a real struggle. He was so unpopular with the people who ran the university that he had no chance of a raise in salary. There was even talk of firing him.

Again, important friends helped. They arranged an interview between Galileo and the leaders of the Republic of Venice, who sponsored the University of

Padua, a city close to the city of Venice. Maybe, when he traveled to Padua, he stayed at a huge inn called The Ox, which had stables for 200 horses.

The interview was a great success. Galileo was clear, lively and intelligent and he was appointed Professor of Mathematics at the University. His salary wasn't a lot better than it had been at Pisa but the chance of a raise was good.

In 1592 Galileo moved his family a hundred and fifty miles across Italy to the city of Padua.

Galileo was a professor at the University of Padua for eighteen years. That university was very different from the one at Pisa. The Venetian Republic believed that scholars should be open-minded and free to argue their ideas, even though the university might disagree with some of them.

Galileo taught astronomy and mathematics. He also taught that science should be more than just thinking about ideas — that science ought to be used to invent practical, useful things. He liked to go into Venice to visit the shops of the craftsmen and the mechanics who manufactured tools and instruments for the Venetian army and navy.

Galileo invented a machine he called a thermoscope, which was the first kind of thermometer.

The thermoscope was a glass bulb and a tube marked with a scale. The open end of the tube was in a liquid. As the liquid in the bottom was heated or

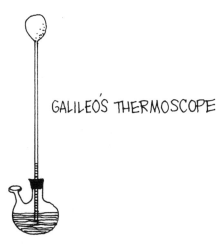

GALILEO'S THERMOSCOPE

cooled, the liquid in the tube rose or fell and the heat could be measured on the scale.

Galileo experimented with lodestones, which are natural magnets, trying in different ways to make their magnetism stronger. He could think of many uses for very strong magnets. (He didn't know that magnets make electric current. Nobody knew that, yet.)

He invented a machine to raise water and irrigate the land. In his patent, Galileo says: "Very easy to use, inexpensive and very convenient, which works pumps using just one horse, spraying the land continuously."

Venice had passed the first patent laws in 1474. A patent grants an inventor the right to market that invention for a certain number of years. As long as the patent is in force, nobody else is allowed to copy the invention, or sell or use it without paying the inventor. (Patent rights are part of the United States Constitution.)

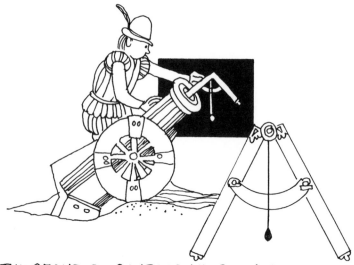

THE GEOMETRIC COMPASS HELPED TO SOLVE
MANY KINDS OF PROBLEMS.

Sometime around 1597, Galileo patented an instrument he called a Geometric and Military Compass.

The compass was a kind of calculating instrument, useful in solving many kinds of problems in geometry and arithmetic. Surveyors wanted it. Builders wanted it. Bankers wanted it. The military wanted it. So Galileo opened a workshop and hired a craftsman to build instruments for sale. The craftsman, Marcantonio Mezzolini, lived with the family.

Several years later Galileo wrote a book on the use of his compass. It was his first book and he wrote it in Italian, for the ordinary people who would be using it.

Books had been published in Italy for more than a hundred years. Earlier books had been written and illustrated by hand, so only rich people could afford them.

Now, printed books were much cheaper. All over Europe, small presses were busy printing books and pamphlets for universities and for readers who wanted to know what was happening in the arts and sciences.

It was unusual for a scholar to write a book in Italian instead of Latin. Galileo dedicated the book to young Cosimo deMedici, who had been a private pupil of his. The Medicis were the most powerful and important family in Italy.

Baldassar Capra, a student at the university, translated the book into Latin, published it and claimed that he had invented the compass. Galileo, enraged, sued Capra, won his case and protected his patent.

Galileo's workshop grew. Selling his instruments was helpful to Galileo who always had problems when it came to managing his family's finances.

When his sisters married, Galileo, as head of the family, was obliged to give them dowries. A dowry was the property a wife brought to her husband when they were married. (In some places, dowries are still the custom.) If the family of the bride was poor, her dowry might be only a cooking pot or a piece of furniture. For an  important person like Galileo, it was a large sum of money. Giving dowries to his sisters left Galileo with big debts.

GALILEO BECOMES A PROFESSOR

Galileo also supported his younger brother, Michelangelo, who was a talented musician. But Michelangelo Galeli couldn't keep a job and Galileo was always paying his bills. (Years later, Michelangelo sent his wife and seven children for Galileo to support.)

Galileo never married, but he had a family. While they were living in Padua, he and his companion, Marina Gamba, had three children. His daughters were called Virginia and Livia, like his sisters. His son was named Vincenzio.

Galileo's salary was raised several times and he was making money from his inventions, but it was not enough. So besides teaching at the university, he made his house into a kind of private boarding school. His students came from rich families all over Europe. More than a dozen of them lived and studied with him.

There wasn't much privacy in those times. Rooms connected to each other without hallways. Bedrooms were also living rooms and kitchens were also dining rooms.

There was plenty to eat — cabbages and carrots, and corn and potatoes from the new world. There was venison and beef, fish and birds. There was always bread and cheap, red wine to drink, because the water was bad and made people sick. Food was often spoiled (No refrigeration, no canning) so cooks made everything very spicy to hide bad tastes. With so many people in the house, there was

always cooking and eating, talking and arguing.

It was a busy, crowded life. Still, Galileo found time to correspond with other scientists and to read and think about different ideas in astronomy. One astronomer's ideas changed his life.

The astronomer's name was Nicholas Copernicus and he had been dead for fifty years.

Galileo said: *The eighteen years I spent at Padua were, without doubt, the best in my life.*

(5)

Three Famous Astronomers

Nicholas Copernicus was born in Poland in 1473. (Twenty years before Columbus discovered America.) He studied mathematics, religion, astronomy and medicine at the University of Cracow and continued his education in Italy. His family was religious and Copernicus became an official of the Church, but his passion was astronomy.

He spent the next thirty years thinking about the ideas of Aristotle and Ptolemy and he decided that their ideas about the universe must be wrong. Wasn't

NICHOLAS COPERNICUS

it simpler to believe that the earth itself was turning, than to believe that everything else in the heavens was turning around the earth?

Copernicus worked out his own idea, that the sun, not the earth, was the center of everything. He believed that the earth was only another planet and that it rotated at the same time it moved around the sun. The sun didn't have to circle the earth to make night and day. Wouldn't the same thing happen if the earth itself turned?

Copernicus believed his ideas were right but he was uneasy about them. They were so different from what appeared to be true that they hardly seemed sensible. He was afraid of being laughed at.

In his writings, Copernicus never discussed matters of religion or faith. He wrote only about astronomy, geometry, and his exact observations of celestial motions.

But his ideas were certainly unlike what the Church taught and Copernicus was a religious man. He was also afraid that the Church wouldn't like his theory because it made the sun, not the earth, the center of the universe.

He wrote his ideas in a long book called *On the Revolution of Heavenly Bodies*. Copernicus finished his book in 1530 but he didn't publish it until 1543, when he was dying.

TYCHO BRAHE

Tycho Brahe, who is usually just called Tycho, was born in Denmark in 1546. His wealthy family wanted him to study law, but he was fascinated by astronomy. Secretly, at night he studied the stars, the constellations, and any astronomical tables he could find.

Later, when he became a full-time astronomer, he had two wonderful observatories. One, on the 2,000 acre island of Sven, between Denmark and Sweden, was called Uraniborg — the Heavenly Castle. (His patron, King Rudolph II, had granted him the rents from all the people who lived on the island.)

The Heavenly Castle was a small city in itself. Other astronomers, instrument makers, assistants and all the people who helped them lived there. Nearby was Tycho's other observatory, the Castle of Stars. (You can visit Uraniborg and see Tycho's observatory and his instruments.)

TYCHO'S OBSERVATORY AT URANIBORG

Tycho made accurate measurements and observations of the motions of the sun, the moon and the planets. He counted and recorded the positions of a thousand stars. He invented and built a number of instruments for making his observations.(One very important instrument was missing. Nobody had invented the telescope yet.)

Tycho believed that the five planets he could see circled the sun. But he also believed that the earth stood still and that the sun circled the earth once a year. (Tycho was stubborn and he fought a lot. He lost the end of his nose in a duel, so he made himself a silver nose to wear.)

Johannes Kepler was born in Germany in 1571. In 1600 he became Tycho's assistant. Tycho and Kepler argued about everything, but when Tycho died he left

JOHANNES KEPLER

Kepler all his papers. Kepler used Tycho's observations to prove that Copernicus was right: the planets, including earth, all moved around the sun.

Kepler figured out three important rules about how the planets move:

1. Their orbits are ellipses, not circles. (The Greeks believed that only circles were perfect.)

2. A planet moves faster when its orbit is closer to the sun.

3. The time it takes for a planet to orbit the sun is related to its distance from the sun. (Earth orbits the sun in about 365 days. That's an earth year. Pluto, the planet farthest from the sun, takes 248 earth years to orbit the sun.)

Kepler was a brilliant mathematician and astronomer. But he also believed in astrology — the idea that the stars predict and control the future of everyone on earth and all the things that happen. In Kepler's times, most people believed that. (They also believed in witchcraft. Kepler's mother was accused of being a witch.)

Galileo, Tycho and Kepler corresponded and exchanged ideas. They agreed among themselves that

Copernicus' ideas were a better explanation of how the world worked than the ideas of Aristotle and Ptolemy. Still, Galileo continued to teach the astronomy of Ptolemy.

By now, Galileo was famous. Students were eager to become his pupils — to live in his house and to exchange ideas with him. His lectures were so popular that famous people traveled from all over Europe to hear him.

In 1604 something amazing happened — a "new star" appeared in the sky. We know now that it was a nova — the light from a far-away sun that had exploded millions of years before. But to the people of that time, who believed in Ptolemy and Aristotle, how was a new star possible? Everything in the heavens was supposed to be perfect and unchanging.

There was so much excitement about the new star that Galileo announced lectures on the subject. The crowds who came were so big that the lectures were given in a hall that held 2,000 people.

Galileo suggested that the new star showed Aristotle's idea of an unchanging heaven to be false. But he was quiet about the ideas of Copernicus, because he felt he had no way to prove them.

 **Galileo said:** *If, in fact, the earth moves, we cannot change nature and have it not move.*

(6)

A New Way of Looking

People had been using eyeglasses to help them see for more than 300 years. At first, there were those who thought eyeglasses should never be worn because they were a kind of trickery. They said that if you could not see something with your eyes alone, it wasn't true. But eyeglasses were so helpful that they became common. Important people even had their portraits painted wearing spectacles, which is another name for eyeglasses.

Glass in the early spectacles was shaped like a lentil bean. The Latin word for a lentil is *lens*. In Galileo's day, all lenses were glass. (Now, lenses are made of other materials, too.)

A lens is a piece of clear stuff — we'll call it glass — with one surface or both surfaces curved.

The curve changes the direction of light rays that come into the glass. Depending on the kind of curve, whatever is seen through the glass looks bigger (or smaller) than it actually is.

If the lens is curved outward, it is called a convex lens.

CONVEX LENS   CONCAVE LENS

If the lens is curved inward, it is called a concave lens.

For hundreds of years, nobody seemed to experiment with the idea of looking through both kinds of lenses together. Then in 1600, the story goes, two children playing in the shop of a Dutch spectacle-maker named Hans Lippershay, put two lenses together and looked through them.

They looked at the weather vane of a church that was some distance away and it looked very big and very near. When Lippershay looked for himself he knew he was seeing something important. He put the lenses together in a tube and started making telescopes, which he called spyglasses.

Lippershay applied to the government of the Netherlands for a patent, but then telescopes began appearing in other places and other people claimed to have invented them. None of them got a patent.

A few weeks after Lippershay applied for his patent, news of the telescope had reached Venice. Then someone offered one for sale to the Venetian Senate. A friar named Paolo Sarpi, who was in charge of scientific matters, looked at a spyglass and decided that it would be useful to have for military purposes, but he was sure that his friend, Galileo Galilei, could make a better one.

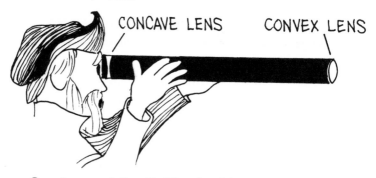

CONCAVE LENS   CONVEX LENS

Sarpi was right. Galileo had heard about the spyglass and found out how it was made. He experimented for a month, trying combinations of lenses until he was satisfied. He made a lead tube about an inch and a half in diameter. He put the concave lens near his eye and the convex lens at the other end. That first tube made things look three times larger.

Finally, Galileo made a spyglass that brought objects thirty times nearer. Galileo later called his instrument a telescopio , from a Greek word meaning "to see at a distance."

THEY SAW SHIPS AND BUILDINGS THAT WERE MILES AWAY.

He took the Senators up into the towers of Venice and showed them distant buildings. He showed them the sails of ships that were miles away.

In August, 1609, Galileo made a gift of his telescope to the Venetian Senate. In thanks, the Senate renewed his professorship for life and doubled his salary. The other professors were really upset. They felt that since Galileo hadn't invented the telescope, he should simply have been paid for it.

The Senate ordered as many telescopes as Galileo's craftsmen could make in his workshop. Everyone who had a telescope enjoyed using it to look around at distant objects. As far as anyone knows, nobody used it to look up.

One winter night at the end of 1609, Galileo took his telescope outside and looked through it at the sky.

Science is full of surprises.

Galileo did not know what he was going to see. He was simply curious about what the telescope *would* see. Night after night he looked.

He saw that the moon was not a smooth, perfect sphere, but that it had mountains and valleys, like the earth.

He saw that the planet Jupiter had "planets" of its own. As he watched and made notes and drawings, they seemed to disappear, then reappear in different places. Galileo realized that he was seeing four moons, orbiting Jupiter.

His drawings showed their changing positions like this:

Goodbye to the idea that all celestial bodies revolved around the earth!

The fact that the moons orbited Jupiter showed something else — that Jupiter was free in space, not encased in a crystal sphere.

Galileo counted more than eighty stars among the three visible stars in the belt of Orion.

He saw that the Milky Way was not just a hazy cloud, but innumerable stars. Wherever he focused his telescope he saw vast crowds of stars.

Galileo announced his discoveries in a twenty-four page pamphlet which he dedicated to Cosimo II, who had been his pupil four years before. Cosimo was now the Grand Duke of Tuscany, The pamphlet was published in March, 1610.

It was called *The Starry Messenger.*

Galileo said: *That which presents itself to mere sight is as nothing compared with the high marvels that learned men discover in the heavens by long and accurate observation.*

(7)

The Starry Messenger

he Starry Messenger was a great success. Only 500 copies were printed and they sold out immediately. Scholars and scientists all over Europe ordered more copies. People were ordering telescopes, too. They wanted the ones made in Galileo's workshop.

Kepler wrote to Galileo. At first he questioned some of the ideas in *The Starry Messenger*. Then Galileo sent him a telescope. After Kepler made his own observations, he published a letter, saying that what Galileo had seen was true. In the letter he said, "Galileo, you have conquered!" The letter meant a lot to Galileo — Kepler was respected all over Europe as an important scientist.

GALILEO'S TELESCOPES WERE VERY BEAUTIFUL

Galileo made an especially beautiful telescope which he presented to Cosimo. He also named the moons of Jupiter after Cosimo's family, calling them the Medicean Planets.

Galileo was planning to ask a big favor of Cosimo. Meanwhile, he kept observing.

He saw that Venus was not an always-glowing object made of something special. It had light and dark phases, like the moon, which showed that Venus orbited the sun the way our earth and its moon do. Its brightness was only reflected sunlight.

He saw that Saturn had a queer shape — a sort of bulge around the middle. He decided that it had a small star attached to each side. We know now that he was seeing Saturn's rings.

GALILEO DREW SATURN
LIKE THIS

Later, he saw spots on the sun.

NEVER NEVER LOOK DIRECTLY AT THE SUN, WITH YOUR EYES OR THROUGH A TELESCOPE OR BINOCULARS. IT CAN HARM YOUR EYES.

Later in his life, Galileo had terrible trouble with his eyes. Probably, that was from the long hours he spent observing the sun through his telescope. Then he found a better way to look at sunspots. In a letter he wrote in 1612, Galileo described it like this:

"Direct the telescope upon the sun as if you were going to observe it. Having focused it, expose a flat white sheet of paper about a foot from the concave lens; upon this will fall a circular image of the sun's disk, with all the spots that are on it arranged and disposed with exactly the same symmetry as in the sun. The more the paper is moved away from the tube, the larger this image will become, and the better the spots will be depicted."

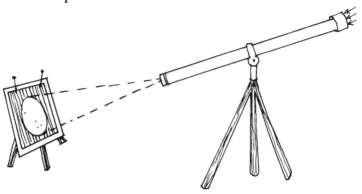

Observers had seen sunspots before. They are visible with eyes alone. (Remember the warning above!) But people assumed that they were seeing objects passing in front of the sun. They did not believe that something as perfect as the sun could have spots.

In Bavaria, Father Christopher Scheiner, a Jesuit astronomer, claimed that he had been the first to discover sunspots. Probably, he and Galileo had seen them at about the same time. But Father Scheiner had published his findings immediately, while Galileo continued to study them. Scheiner insisted that the spots were small planets passing in front of the sun.

Galileo studied sunspots for two years before he

GALILEO'S DRAWINGS OF SUNSPOTS

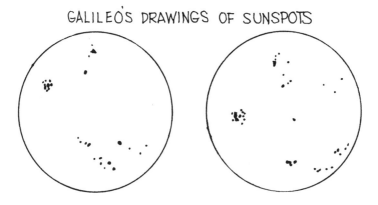

published a paper called *Letter on Sunspots*. He noticed that the spots seemed to move across the surface of the sun, from west to east and that they drifted from south to north. He also noticed that some were big and some were small. Their shapes changed, so they could not be moons, which are always round. Galileo decided that the spots were more like storm clouds on earth than anything else.

He tracked them over long periods of time, which convinced him that the sun turned, like the earth. He figured out that the sun took twenty-seven days to make a complete turn on its axis.

Scientists and philosophers who believed that Aristotle could not be wrong were increasingly angry at Galileo. Some said that moons around Jupiter and spots on the sun were defects in the lenses of his telescopes. They even accused him of purposely putting the spots in his telescopes to deceive people.

THE STARRY MESSENGER

Some admitted that there might be mountains and craters on the moon, but then they explained that the whole moon was encased in a giant crystal globe, so it was still perfect.

Some said that nothing was true unless you could see it with your eyes alone. And that if you could only see a star or a moon through a telescope, its light did not reach earth and therefore, it did not exist.

Galileo said that if by day, you could see the writing on a building miles away through the spyglass, and if by night you could see the moons of Jupiter through the spyglass, why, if it saw truthfully on earth, why not truthfully in the sky?

Some refused to even look through a telescope.

Some said that Galileo was a dangerous man because he contradicted the Church teachings that earth and its inhabitants were the center of the universe.

Galileo was tired of teaching at the university. The more famous he became, the angrier the other professors were. Working with them was uncomfortable. And he was tired of the hours he spent with the private pupils who crowded his house and ate at his table.

He thought of Copernicus, spending undisturbed years thinking out his theories.

He thought of Tycho, counting the stars and inventing wonderful instruments to use in his observatory.

He thought of Kepler, working quietly with Tycho's papers.

COSIMO II

Naming the Medicean planets after the Grand Duke, and giving him a beautiful telescope were part of a plan. Galileo wanted to leave the university. He wanted to stop teaching. He wanted to spend all his time thinking, writing, and possibly inventing. He could do this if Cosimo became his patron.

A patron would support Galileo, give him a salary and pay all his bills, both for living and working. Galileo would be free of any chores.

In June, 1610, his wish came true. Cosimo appointed Galileo Chief Mathematician of the University of Pisa and Philosopher of the Grand Duke. He didn't have to teach or even live at the university. His salary was a thousand scudi a year, for life and he looked forward to years of thinking, experimenting and writing.

What Galileo didn't consider was that he would no longer be under the protection of the Venetian Republic, which didn't frown on new ideas.

In 1610, when he was forty-six, Galileo moved to Florence.

Galileo's young son, Vincenzio, stayed in Padua with his mother, Marina Gamba. Galileo's daughters moved to Florence with him and his mother. But Galileo's mother was so disagreeable that it was not a happy household. Galileo hated the turmoil. In 1613 Galileo sent the girls to school at the Convent of San Matteo, in Arcetri, a beautiful town in the hills above Florence. As soon as they were sixteen, both girls became nuns. Virginia became  Sister Maria Celeste. Livia became Sister Arcangela. (Marina Gamba later married. She and Galileo stayed friends.)

The professors at Pisa and Padua were more and more jealous of Galileo's success so they were more determined than ever to prove that Aristotle was right and Galileo was wrong. Now, Galileo decided that he needed important people on his side. In 1611 he traveled to Rome, taking one of his telescopes with him.

He met with the astronomers of the College of Rome and their leader, Father Clavius and he left the telescope with them. Night after night they watched for themselves.

They became convinced that Galileo's observations were true but they didn't think those observations proved Copernicus to be right. They still supported Aristotle and Ptolemy.

Galileo met other important people while he was in Rome. He had an audience with Pope Paul V. He met Cardinal Bellarmine and Cardinal Barbarini, who later became Pope Urban VIII. All of them liked Galileo and were impressed by his ideas.

One night a banquet was held in Galileo's honor and he was elected to the Academy of the Lynxes, the first scientific honor society. The society was dedicated to the promotion of new ideas, especially in science. At that time most people, even scholars, thought that astronomy wasn't useful for much, except, perhaps, predicting the seasons.

When he returned to Florence, Galileo was sure that the important people he had seen understood his thinking. Now, he thought, he could openly support Copernicus.

 **Galileo said:** *Men are forced into strange fancies by attempting to measure the whole universe by means of their tiny scale.*

(8)

Galileo Loves A Fight

G alileo was not the kind of scientist who spent all his time studying and working quietly by himself. He loved a fight. He enjoyed poking fun at his enemies and he had a real talent for making people angry at him. He was so witty and clever with words that he usually won any argument, which did not make him popular with the people who were arguing on the other side.

His enemies — the professors at Pisa and Padua and their friends in Rome — formed a secret society called the Liga. The object of the Liga was to bring Galileo down. The head of the Liga was a large, unpleasant scholar named Ludovico delle Colombe, who always lost any scientific debates he had with Galileo. Colombe was determined that if he couldn't get the best of Galileo in matters of science, he would challenge his religious beliefs. Galileo called the members of the Liga "pigeons." (Colombe means "pigeon" in Italian.)

Galileo always seemed to be fighting to defend Copernicus and his system of how the universe worked. Really, Galileo was defending the right of scientists to express their ideas about science, even if those ideas were different from the ideas of Aristotle and the ideas of the Church.

In most of Europe, Galileo and his arguments were hardly noticed, except by scholars.

From 1612 to 1648 war raged across the continent.

The war wasn't over trade routes or control of the new lands that had been discovered overseas. It was over religious differences and the power of princes and their diplomats. Neighboring nations either tried to conquer each other, or tried to keep from being conquered.

They hired mercenary soldiers, who fought for pay. The soldiers preyed on the people in the towns and in the country and made their lives miserable. By the time the Thirty Years War was over, both the towns and the countryside were in ruins. The crops were unfarmed and crafts and industries had been destroyed. Science was the last thing on most people's minds.

 **Galileo said:** *Since no two truths can contradict one another, the position of Copernicus and the Bible must be perfectly harmonious.*

Trouble Begins

The Grand Duke Cosimo liked to give dinners where scholars and scientists could discuss the new ideas of the times. His mother, the Grand Duchess Christina, enjoyed the discussions and often entered into them. At one reception, there was an argument between Cosimo Boscaglia, a professor at the University of Pisa and a Benedictine monk named Benedetto Castelli, a friend of Galileo's. Castelli had been one of Galileo's pupils. (At the time of the dinner, Galileo was sick in bed.)

Boscaglia said that the Copernican theory had to

be wrong because it contradicted the Bible. Castelli said that science should be discussed on its own, not as an exact reading of the Bible. As Castelli was leaving, the Grand Duchess called him back to question him about Copernicus, Galileo, and the Scriptures. Madame Christina argued that the Holy Scriptures contradicted Galileo's ideas.

When Castelli reported the evening's events to Galileo, Galileo wrote him a letter, and another, longer one to the Grand Duchess, explaining that science did not contradict the Bible — that there must be two separate languages — the language of the Bible and the language of science.

He wrote that the Bible was written so that ordinary people could understand it in their own terms. When the Bible says, "The sun stood still" or, "The sun also rises and the sun goes down," that is how it appears to happen. In Biblical times, it could not be explained in any other way.

In science, though, the language must be exact. It must explain, carefully, what actually happens. He said, "There is only one truth, but two ways of telling it. "

In his *Letter to the Grand Duchess*, Galileo asked, "Why has God given humans senses, brains and the power to reason, if not to figure out scientific truths?" And he wrote that the Bible teaches how one goes to Heaven, not how the heavens go.

Galileo wanted the support of the Church for science but Kepler felt that Galileo was making a mistake. He wanted Galileo to leave it alone — that the argument could only bring trouble. Kepler said that if there was no argument, scientists could be free to study and experiment. Arguing with the Church was dangerous.

The argument wasn't just between Galileo and the Church. Different groups in the Church disagreed among themselves.

The Jesuits supported Galileo for many years. Then, in an argument about comets, they turned against him.

The Benedictines were his friends.

But those who belonged to the Order of the Dominicans were absolutely opposed to any new ideas.

One of them, Tommaso Cassini, preached a loud sermon, shouting that Galileo should not spread ideas that contradicted the Bible.

Supporters of Galileo demanded an apology.

Another Dominican, Father Lorini, kept up the attack. He sent a forged, misleading copy of Galileo's letter to Castelli to the Inquisition in Rome.

The Inquisition was a group in the Church that investigated reports of heresy, which meant speaking against what the Church believed to be true.

After they had read the letter, the Inquisition said they had no objections to it. Galileo thought they had no objection to his ideas, so he could go ahead with his work. He did not realize that there was a battle going on between those who translated the Bible literally and those who wanted the Church to be open-minded about new ideas.

The more his powerful friends inside the Church supported him, the more the other side argued against him.

Two Cardinals, Maffeo Barbarini and Roberto Bellarmine were his friends. They advised Galileo to stick to his science and not argue theology with Church leaders.

Bellarmine said that there was no danger for

mathematicians to say that the earth moves and the sun stands still. But to wish to prove that the sun is in the center of the heavens and turns upon itself, and that the earth is just a planet whirling around the sun, is dangerous because it makes the Scriptures seem false. To say that it appears that the sun is in the center and that the earth is in the heavens, turning around the sun, is different from proving that fact.

In 1616, Pope Paul V asked Cardinal Bellarmine to meet Galileo and warn him not to teach or write or even think about agreeing with the Copernican theory, or he would be called before the Inquisition.

Galileo had no choice. He agreed. Years later, there was a lot of trouble about what really happened at this meeting.

In the autumn of 1618, three comets appeared, one

after another, each one brighter than the last.

Comets were frightening. Most people thought they were omens of something terrible to come — an earthquake or the plague. Everywhere, they watched and whispered and wondered about them. Scientists all over Europe argued about the comets.

Galileo was very ill and in bed that autumn, so he could not make the long observations he wanted to make.

Nobody knew what comets were.

Aristotle had said that comets were in the air that surrounded the earth, rising to the sphere of fire, where they were ignited until they blazed.

Tycho had said that comets were far above the moon, far above Aristotle's sphere of fire. He didn't say what they were made of.

Galileo thought that comets might be something like rainbows, caused by the sun reflecting on air that rose to great distances high above the earth. (That sounded a lot like Aristotle's theory.)

Now we know that comets are made of ice, dust, rocks and gas. We know that far out in space, out past the planet Pluto, there is a huge cloud of comets orbiting the solar system. We think that once in a while, some faraway star gives a push or a pull that yanks a comet out of the cloud and sends it moving into orbit around the sun.

So Galileo, like Aristotle, wasn't always right. He wasn't right about comets and his ideas were wrong about what causes the tides. He thought the tides were caused by two earthly motions — the earth turning on its axis and at the same time moving around the sun. (Now we know that the moon's gravitational pull causes the tides.)

Galileo got into an argument about comets with a Jesuit priest named Horatio Grassi. They argued in letters and articles, both writing under assumed names, even though most readers knew who the writers were. Galileo's article was called *The Assayer*. He was wrong about comets, but some of the things he wrote in *The Assayer* are some of the most important ideas in science.

Think about this yourself.

When you are describing something, is it enough

to say that it is big or small? Is it as big as a house? What kind of house? A cottage or an apartment house?

If you say that something is small, what does "small" mean? As small as a green pea? As small as a mouse?

Is it near, or far? As near as your front door? Or as near as the traffic light down the street?

Is something as far as the next town or as far as the moon?

What is its shape? Round, square, long, short?

Is it still or is it moving? If it's moving, how fast?

Is there one thing, or a few, or many? How many?

Galileo wrote that you must observe, compare and measure — that the book of nature is written in mathematics.

Galileo spent the next few years working on inventions — a telescope that could be used in ships and an instrument for finding longitude at sea. (Nobody had been able to make such an instrument, so sailors often did not know where on the oceans they were.)

Between illnesses he worked on his microscope. At first he found that while the tube of a telescope for looking at the stars needed to be only two feet long, his instrument for making small objects look big needed to be four or six feet long. Then, between 1619 and 1624 he found a way to make microscopes of a smaller size. Galileo called his microscopes "occhialini." When he first looked through his microscope, he wrote, "I have seen flies that look as big as lambs and I have learned that they are covered all over with hair."

FERDINAND II

In 1621 Galileo's good friend, Grand Duke Cosimo died and his son, Ferdinand, became Grand Duke. Ferdinand supported Galileo and tried to protect him but he was not as strong or as powerful as his father.

In 1624 Cardinal Barbarini became Pope Urban VIII. Galileo went to Rome several times to visit him. They had been friends for a long time.

Galileo asked permission to write a book, comparing the ideas of Ptolemy and Copernicus. He promised that the book would be absolutely fair to both sides. The Pope agreed. Galileo thought the Pope was agreeing that now, Catholic scientists could study Copernican ideas. He misunderstood.

When Galileo finished his book, *A Dialogue on Two World Systems*, he dedicated it to the Pope.

The *Dialogue* was written as if it were a four day discussion of the two chief systems of the world.

There are three characters in the discussion.

FRONTESPIECE OF THE *DIALOGUE*

One is a nobleman from Florence, who defends Copernicus.

One is a nobleman from Venice, who is open-minded.

The third, Simplicio, believes absolutely that the earth is the center of the universe.

The *Dialogue* was published in February, 1632.

It was written in Italian, so anyone with an education could read it. The *Dialogue* was read and applauded not only in Italy, but all over Europe. Galileo was flooded with letters, saying how clearly he had explained things about the new worlds, how sensible the new theories were, and how he had made readers see that the old truths were not truths at all.

In August, the book's printer was ordered to stop printing and selling the book.

In October, Galileo was ordered to come to Rome and stand trial before the Inquisition. He was sixty-eight years old.

 **Galileo said:** *The universe is written in the language of mathematics.*

(10)

The Trial of Galileo

When the summons to appear before the Inquisition came, Galileo was very, very sick. His doctors wrote to the Pope, saying that he was old and very ill, and that traveling to Rome at this time might kill him.

The Pope threatened that if he did not come on his own accord, he would be brought to Rome in chains.

The Grand Duke provided a litter for him — a portable bed, surrounded by heavy curtains. He provided horses and a driver. In the bitter, February weather, Galileo was carried in the litter, all the way from Florence to Rome. The roads were awful and the

clumsy, wooden wheels sank into deep ruts. Besides, there was plague through the countryside and the litter was stopped again and again at places that were quarantined. The cold, miserable trip took twenty-five days.

Galileo was supposed to go directly to prison, but instead he was allowed to stay at the palace of Francesco Niccolini, the Grand Duke's ambassador to Rome, on the condition that he did not leave the palace or have visitors.

Galileo was in despair. All his writings and his studies to reveal scientific truths had come to nothing. He was especially bitter that his enemies had accused him of heresy, even though he was, and had always been a devout Catholic.

Part of Galileo's problem was that the Pope was in a lot of trouble himself.

The Spanish ambassador had attacked him for protecting heretics because he supported France and Sweden in the war against Spain and the Holy Roman Empire.

In Rome he was accused of favoring his family because he had promoted three nephews to important positions.

Galileo's enemies had convinced the Pope that Simplicio, one of the characters in *The Dialogue* was really a caricature of himself, humiliating him by showing him to be stupid.

The Pope decided that punishing someone as important as Galileo would show his power and demonstrate that he would even sacrifice an old friend to defend the Church from heresy.

The Pope's mathematician, Fra Castelli, warned the Pope that the Church was endangering its reputation. What if Galileo's ideas proved to be true? He said, "The Church can forbid men to write, but it cannot make the earth either stand still or move."

Galileo's friends told him that the time for argument was over. He must stop trying to convince the Church that his reasons for supporting Copernicus were scientific, not religious. They advised him not to bring up those arguments in the trial.

His accusers were determined to trap him. They wanted him to admit that he had broken the promise he had made to Cardinal Bellarmine years ago, not to believe, defend or teach the ideas of Copernicus.

Being brought before the Inquisition was terrifying.

GIORDANO BRUNO

At the beginning of the century, an Italian philosopher named Giordano Bruno had been condemned by the Inquisition and burned to death as a heretic because he said that the stars were like the sun and were enormous distances away from us. He said that the universe had no beginning or end and that space was infinite. (What ideas!)

Just before Bruno died, he said, "The time will come when all men will see as I see."

Galileo had no intention of becoming a martyr — someone who died for a belief. What he wanted was to be free and allowed to continue his work in peace.

He appeared before the Inquisition four times. After the first trial he was kept in prison, even though it was in a comfortable room.

At the second trial he confessed that he had argued for Copernicus's theory and that he had mistakenly taken pleasure in showing himself cleverer than other people.

At the third trial he said that he had simply forgotten his promise to Cardinal Bellarmine.

At the fourth trial he thought that he was being threatened with torture if he did not confess, so he signed a paper saying that the accusations were true. Two days later he was sentenced.

Galileo was forced to recite, on his knees, a long

document saying that he now, and always had, believed all that was taught by the Church. The document went on: "I must wholly forsake the false opinion that the sun is the center of the world and moves not and that the earth is not the center of the world and moves."

People who were at the trial told that when Galileo struggled up from his knees he tapped the earth with his foot and whispered, "Eppur si muove," which means, "And yet it does move."

Three of the ten Cardinals who were the judges did not come to the sentencing and refused to sign the verdict.

The Dialogue was burned and all Galileo's books were banned.

In June, 1633, Galileo was sentenced to prison for life.

Galileo said: *l hold the sun to be situated motionless in the center of the revolution of the celestial orbs, while the earth rotates on its axis and revolves around the sun.*

(11)

Galileo's Last Years

Galileo knew that even though *The Dialogue* was forbidden in Italy, that wasn't the end of it. He knew that because of his reputation it would be published and read all over Europe. Outside of Italy, the Pope's ban meant nothing.

The Pope did not plan to keep Galileo in prison and he was allowed to go back to the palace of Ambassador Niccolini. But Galileo wanted to leave Rome forever. In a few days the favor was granted and he was allowed to move to Siena, to the home of his friend, Archbishop Piccolomini. The Archbishop was happy to have him. He wanted Galileo to feel that his palace wasn't a prison, but a place where he could rest, read and think, and have friends to talk to.

This irritated Galileo's enemies, who felt that he wasn't being punished enough. They argued that he had no right to continue the discussion of his ideas, just as if he had not been condemned at all! They said he was still a dangerous man who was spreading dangerous ideas. They wanted him to be in some out-of-the-way place, that was more like a real prison.

Galileo actually liked this idea. He asked if he could move to a small farm he owned at Arcetri, in the hills behind Florence, close to the Convent where his daughters lived. The Pope granted him permission to move to Arcetri as long as he lived in solitude, with no visitors.

SISTER MARIA CELESTE

Galileo particularly loved his elder daughter, Sister Maria Celeste and he was happy to be near her. He moved to the farm in December, 1633. The following April, Maria Celeste died. His other daughter and his son, Vincenzio were no substitute for her. He sat for hours, playing his lute.

Then Galileo went back to work. His friends tried over and over to free him from his house arrest. They were never able to do that, but they smuggled letters in and out, so he was able to have discussions with scholars who were interested in his ideas.

Gradually, he began to have visitors from all over Europe.

The great English poet, John Milton, visited Galileo on his travels through Europe.

So did the English philosopher, Thomas Hobbes. Hobbes thought that matter and its motion were as

JOHN MILTON

THOMAS HOBBES

83

much a subject for philosophy as for science and he admired Galileo for being a scientist and a philosopher.

Galileo's friends from all over Italy came to talk and eat with him. And all the time, he was working on his last book, *Discourses and Mathematical Demonstrations Relating to Two New Sciences Concerning Mechanics*. (The two new sciences were force and motion. Usually, the book is just called, *"Discourses on Two New Sciences."*) The book summed up his experiments and all his ideas.

Discourses is about acceleration, (which means speeding up or slowing down), and about light, sound and heat. It's about how things move and how they fall. It's about mathematics and experiments and infinity. It's about gravity, even though nobody knew what that was.

(Isaac Newton, who was born the year Galileo died, built his theory about gravitation on those ideas. He also used Galileo's work on moving things to state his

ISAAC NEWTON

Laws of Motion, which describe why things move or don't move, what starts or stops them , and how fast they will go.)

In 1637, after years of troubles with his eyes, Galileo went blind.

Now, because he was blind and in such poor health, he was allowed to have two pupils, who lived with him and were his friends and assistants.

Both became famous physicists. Vincenzio Viviani wrote a biography of Galileo. Evangelista Torricelli invented the barometer and a microscope and made improvements on the telescope.

Now, the letters Galileo exchanged with friends and other scientists were not fierce arguments. He even accepted some of Aristotle's reasoning and logic. But he said that logic must be combined with mathematical proof — that there is no middle ground between truth and falsity.

Galileo kept thinking and inventing.

Since 1604 a grand prize had been offered for the invention of a machine that would help sailors find longitude at sea.

Galileo had worked on the problem for years. At first he invented a helmet with a telescope attached, to be worn by a navigator, sitting in a chair set in gimbals to keep the chair horizontal. That idea wasn't practical.

In the last years of his life he was thinking again about how to measure time when suddenly he saw the

connection between the motion of a pendulum and a clock. His son, Vincenzio, often visited him and together they worked on the idea. They wanted to build the clock secretly. Nobody had yet found a way to determine longitude at sea, so nobody had collected the prize. (The prize was finally won when an Englishman named John Harrison invented a sea-going clock called a chronoscope, in 1759.)

Galileo thought his clock might be the answer but the clock was never finished. Vincenzio was building it himself when on January 8, 1642, Galileo died, a month before his seventy-eighth birthday.

The Grand Duke wanted to give him a magnificent

GALILEO FINALLY CONNECTED THE SWING OF A PENDULUM WITH TIMEKEEPING.

tomb, but the Inquisition said that was not fitting for a condemned heretic. So Galileo was buried quietly in the family church.

In the next century he was moved to a grand tomb in the Church of Santa Croce, in Florence.

In 1822 the Church lifted the ban on Galileo's books. Now the works of Galileo, Kepler and Copernicus were all open to everyone. (By this time, everyone knew, anyway, that the earth was a planet, orbiting the sun.)

In 1979 Pope John Paul II said that the Church had wronged Galileo.

In 1984, almost 350 years after Galileo died, the

Pope's Academy of Sciences in Rome cleared Galileo's name absolutely and said that his arguments were true.

Now, imagine how Galileo would enjoy the space-craft Galileo as it voyages for years around the planet Jupiter, exploring the moons he was first to see. There they are, close up, Ganymede, Callisto, Europa and Io. And beyond them, other planets, other moons and the universe he surely imagined.

As his good friend Viviani wrote, when Galileo died, "He rendered up his soul to his Creator, sending it, as he liked to believe, to enjoy and to watch from a closer vantage point those eternal and immutable marvels which he, by means of a fragile device, had brought closer to our mortal eyes with such eagerness and impatience."

 **Galileo said:** *The Bible intends to teach how one goes to Heaven, not how the heavens go.*

EPILOGUE

Galileo is buried in the Church of Santa Croce, in Florence.

But a glass and marble casket in the Florence Museum of the Story of Science displays one of his fingers. The inscription reads: This is the finger with which the illustrious hand covered the heavens and indicated their immense space. It pointed to new stars with the marvellous instrument, made of glass, and revealed them to the senses.

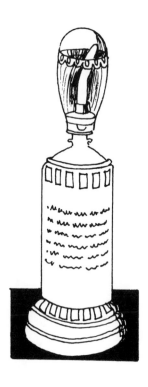

INDEX

INDEX

INDEX